Autism and Play

of related interest

Asperger's Syndrome
A Guide for Parents and Professionals
Tony Attwood
ISBN 1 85302 577 1

Small Steps Forward
Using Games and Activities to Help your Pre-School Child with Special Needs
Sarah Newman
ISBN 1 85302 643 3

Parents' Education as Autism Therapists
Applied Behaviour Analysis in Context
Edited by Mickey Keenan, Ken P. Kerr and Karola Dillenburger
ISBN 1 85302 778 2

A Positive Approach to Autism
Stella Waterhouse
ISBN 1 85302 808 8

Children with Autism, Second Edition
Diagnosis and Intervention to Meet Their Needs
Colwyn Trevarthen, Kenneth Aitken, Despina Papoudi and Jacqueline Robarts
ISBN 1 85302 555 0

Autism: An Inside-Out Approach
An Innovative Look at the Mechanics of 'Autism' and its Development 'Cousins'
Donna Williams
ISBN 1 85302 387 6

Autism and Sensing
The Unlost Instinct
Donna Williams
ISBN 1 85302 612 3

Through the Eyes of Aliens
A Book About Autistic People
Jasmine Lee O'Neill
ISBN 1 85302 710 3

Pretending to be Normal
Living with Asperger's Syndrome
Liane Holliday Willey
ISBN 1 85302 749 9

To Nadja Mac

Autism and Play

Jannik Beyer and Lone Gammeltoft

Foreword by Demetrious Haracopos

Jessica Kingsley Publishers
London and Philadelphia

The right of Jannik Beyer and Lone Gammeltoft to be identified as authors of this work has been asserted by them in accordance with the Copyright, Designs and Patents Act 1988.

First published in Danish in 1998 by the *Videnscenter for Autisme*, Denmark. Translated by Kirsten Callesen.

First published in English in 2000 by Jessica Kingsley Publishers Ltd, 116 Pentonville Road, London N1 9JB, England and 325 Chestnut Street, Philadelphia PA 19106, USA.

www.jkp.com

Library of Congress Cataloging in Publication Data
A CIP catalog record for this book is available from the Library of Congress

British Library Cataloguing in Publication Data
A CIP catalogue record for this book is available from the British Library

ISBN 1 85302 845 2 pb

Printed and Bound in Great Britain by
Athenaeum Press, Gateshead, Tyne and Wear

Contents

Foreword

Today, there is considerable literature and research on the problems and needs of autism. While knowledge about diagnosis, theoretical understanding and intervention possibilities is growing steadily, there is little literature on autism and play. It is harder still to find information about the functions and qualities of play among children with autism, and about how one can best enhance play skills.

It is a common claim in the literature that one of the major symptoms and problems that characterizes people with autism is that these children lack the ability and interest to become involved in play activities. Their play with toys and other objects is non-goal directed and often unusual. They usually demonstrate a lack of interest in interacting and playing with other children. Some children with autism will spend hours on end on the same monotonous and repetitive activity, making it difficult for others to involve them in meaningful activities.

In this light, one may ask: Can children with autism learn to play? Can these children be motivated to enjoy taking part in play activities? Can play open new developmental paths for autistic children? These are the central themes in this important book, written by two experienced and competent professionals, who for more than two decades have devoted their careers to working with children with this disability.

The authors provide a coherent description and explanation of the connection between theoretical understanding and educational intervention. They have also succeeded in providing a sound theoretical framework, in accordance with current knowledge and understanding of autism, to explain the development of play among non-autistic children as compared to children with autism. At the same time, this theoretical framework serves as an ideal platform for describing intervention strategies in this exciting educational area.

This book is particularly valuable and special in that the authors provide professionals and parents with focused and detailed ideas for the planning of play activities – ideas that can be applied directly. The excellent photographs supplement the educational strategies. The authors describe how even very low-functioning children with autism can benefit from play activities.

Those who decide to have *Autism and Play* on their bookshelves will find inspiration in this excellent book. I have observed some of the children who the authors have worked with, and I was elated to see that autistic children are indeed able to learn how to play in well structured and clearly defined situations. More importantly, however, I saw not only that they can be motivated and actively involved in various play activities, but that they truly enjoy it.

This book is essential reading and a valuable source of inspiration for professionals and parents who are

looking for creative and practical ideas for play
activities for children with autism.

Dr Demetrious Haracopos

*Director: The Danish Information
and Training Center for Autism*

Preface

That playing is a crucial factor of a child's development is unquestionable. Play gives joy, the essence of play is meaningful and it contributes to the general development of the different aspects in the personality. Playing also occupies a great part of the normal child's life and most people recall their childhood as a playful time.

Children do not all have the same opportunities for play. Some children are cut off from playing due to social factors – other children are cut off due to their different psychological functioning. Our sentiments are aroused when we hear of children in the third world having their days crammed with work that belongs to the adult world, but we do not pay attention to just how often children with reduced capacity in our part of the world have their days crammed with training programs – even if it is with the best intentions.

Children with autism belong to the latter category. This group of children do not naturally realize the potential of play and they are often referred to as children who are unable to play.

Our objective in this book is to bring into focus the right to play for all children despite their different abilities.

Children with autism may benefit immensely from play and we have been astonished by the social competence shown by many of the children, when they have been guided into the world of play.

It is our responsibility to design and set up an environment for these children based on their particular needs in play.

This book emanates from years of experience and time spent with children with autism. The project for studying children with autism at play was initially scheduled to last a few years, but it continues still, as the children constantly introduce us to new methods and perspectives for playing.

We want to share our experiences with parents and professionals and raise awareness of the theoretical importance of autism and play.

We wish to thank the children and parents at Broendagerskolen for their inspiration and participation.

A special thank you to teacher Marianne S. Nordenhof for her creative cooperation in the development of group play and Social Stories, and to Tove Schultz, Mette Deibjerg, Lone Beyer and Jens Laursen for their constructive criticism of the scripts.

August 1st 1999
Jannik Beyer and Lone Gammeltoft

Introduction

A group of children are playing. Some of them are fighting while others laugh; one child is standing by himself – he seems to need a playmate. Is something wrong? How does it feel to be left out like this?

We think about what we see and use our imaginations –
these thoughts and images are part of a shared social
understanding. A five-year-old child and an adult
would usually get the same impression of the scene in a
picture like this. Perhaps this is the secret behind our
way of interpreting and understanding the world. We
can pick up immediately on the social cues and can gain
a common understanding of the social context.

What would happen if a child with autism saw the
same picture? Would this child instantly notice the
interactions and relationships in the group of children,
and would a child with autism express thoughts on
what the other children might be experiencing and
feeling? Or would a child with autism become
preoccupied with a single detail in the picture – the ball,
the teddybear or the boy with glasses?

The answer is not easy – children with autism do
have a different outlook on the world. This outlook
varies from child to child and no two children are the
same. Do children with autism play at all with other
children?

OBJECTIVES AND WAYS OF PRESENTING THE PROBLEM

The fact that children with autism do not play in a varied and spontaneous way should not mean that play activities cannot be a source of personal development. Children with autism can learn how to play, if parents and teachers become aware of the rules which govern play – like every human activity, play has its own hidden set of rules.

The aim of this book is to make explicit the basis and potential of play activities for children with autism.

We have worked for many years on the development of communication – that has many links with the development of play. Children with autism do not communicate like other children. They need to learn strategies to do so, and communication is still one of the most crucial and rewarding areas for educational intervention. Like communication, play activity is a difficult but rewarding area of intervention.

THE STRUCTURE OF THIS BOOK

The first part of this book gives a brief overview of autistic syndrome in the light of the early development of non-autistic children, as well as a presentation of the rules and basis of play.

The final part, which is more practically oriented, provides different examples and draws out strategies for creating play sequences. These sequences are designed to enhance children's play. To construct actual play sequences for individuals, it is crucial to evaluate each child's capacity. There is a questionnaire in the appendix for systematically recording and evaluating play.

The direct source of inspiration for this book is the children. Through their interaction, they have generated the actual script for the book. Therefore it seemed natural to use photographs of the children to illustrate the play sequences.

Children usually experience and organize their world in more than one dimension at the same time. We call these dimensions 'the physical approach' and 'the social approach' to the world. For a non-autistic child, the two dimensions are fully integrated in their access to information. For children with autism, information is often processed through only one dimension, the physical approach.

It is difficult to explain the social dimension to a child with autism – we tend to experience this dimension internally. We get to know the social sphere through our own emotions.

With play it is possible to bring together 'the physical dimension' and 'the social dimension'.

If we respect and support the child's perspective, play activities can be an opening into the social dimension.

The non-autistic child learns social insight and understanding through play. We are convinced that play also has great potential for children with autism. Most children play in a spontaneous and explorative manner. It is up to us to be creative in order to make the development of play possible for a child with autism.

We have been pleasantly surprised to witness children's motivation and joy in playing together, as well as their discovery of social interaction.

To share, to show happiness, to tease and to be annoyed are all facets of human interaction. Play activities provide a framework for children to experience these emotions in themselves as well as in other people. Such emotions can be very hard for children with autism to relate to.

HOW DO WE UNDERSTAND AUTISM?

The best way to understand autism is to hold on to the impression each autistic child gives you when you meet him. A disability related to communication and social interaction is not one-sided; it exists in the relationships between people. We must try, therefore, to understand how these ways of relating come about.

We are surprised by the lack of social and communicative competence of autistic people, only because we take this competence for granted. We assume that children approach us with an ability to communicate and to interact socially. Perhaps we should be surprised instead by the fact that so many children are born with this natural ability.

We may be impressed by the skills a non-autistic child develops when he begins to go to school: reading, writing, maths, and so on; but we tend to forget all the other skills a child acquires during early interaction, which he learns long before beginning school.

Autism begins to manifest before the age of three, and some of the most central problems in autism are reflected in the abilities a non-autistic child would master before reaching the age of 18–24 months. A deep insight into early development is, therefore, a prerequisite for understanding autism.

The British psychologist, David Ricks (1976) illustrated how fundamental this problem is. Ricks gathered three groups of children without a spoken language: six children with autism, six children with a general learning disability and six children without a disability.

The children were presented with four incidents – and their reactions were taped on a cassette player:

1. The child was presented with his favourite dish.

2. The dish was kept out of reach from the child.

3. The child saw his mother again after being separated.

4. A balloon was blown up.

Then the mothers were asked to listen to the tapes and describe what they heard. Everyone found it easy to interpret the reactions of those with or without general learning disabilities on the tapes; but as the children's reactions were quite similar, the mothers had difficulties identifying their own child.

For the mothers of autistic children, it was a different matter. These mothers were able to identify their own child on tape and interpret their reaction.

There are some thought-provoking points to Ricks' study:

- Children with autism either fail – or very early on, lose – a normal child's innate ability to express universal emotions (emotions which may be understood by all people).

- Children with autism do express feelings – and by no means in a random manner.

- Children with autism need other people to know them thoroughly, in order to interpret accurately the way they express their emotions.

- It is often the parents, who relate intimately to their child, who have the best means to interpret his reactions.

It may be easy to understand a non-autistic child's expressions, but specific knowledge and experience is needed for understanding a child with autism – and then this understanding only relates to the particular child. Two children with autism do not express their feelings in the same manner. Thus we address a communication problem that is shared by the adult and the child.

NOTE

The pronouns 'he' and 'she' are used interchangeably in the text.

PART 1

Autism and early development

Infantile autism is a pervasive developmental disorder. Autism is defined in terms of three areas, often referred to as the triad:

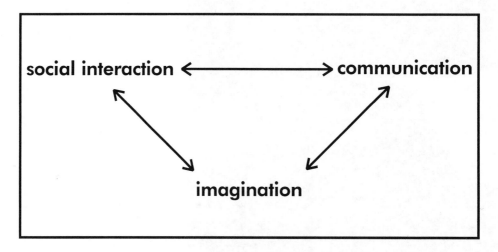

Social interaction, communication and imagination are the principal elements in play activities. It comes as no surprise therefore that children with autism engage in play activities in an unusual way.

But how do each of the three elements of the triad influence play?

PROBLEM AREA 1
Social interaction

From birth, the infant can distinguish between images of life and death, and human and non-human qualities. As early as the second month after birth, the infant's reactions to objects and humans become clearly differentiated. The child uses physical objects as a source of sensory information or of interest and as possible 'catching objects', 'chewing objects' or 'kicking objects'. When communicating with humans on the other hand, the infant uses bodily movements and facial expressions.

Quite a lot of theories have been proposed on how a child acquires her initial experiences and how she organizes and connects different images, in order to create a meaningful understanding of the world. There is now a consensus that a child's understanding is connected to both her intellect and emotions. It is believed that social interaction, emotions, early experiences and cognition are all part of the child's early processing and integration of experiences.

Two worlds

The infant gains knowledge of herself as well as her environment through varied but systematic exploration. When we think about early play, we think of the exploratory 'rattling, kicking, dragging, sucking on' world, where everything has a cause and effect. In this world, the child repeats the same act again and again – every time with the same result. When she bangs the rattle against the bedframe, it makes a sound. When she repeats the banging, it makes the same sound. When she bangs the rattle against her head it hurts. When she lets go of the rattle, it disappears, and so on.

This is a world of defined rules which the child slowly learns to master, although the impersonal world of objects is not the most important one to the infant.

There is another world – a 'communicating with' world. A world that consists of Mum, Dad, siblings, and so forth. This world is more attractive to the child and is explored enthusiastically. The 'social' world also has its own kind of regularity.

Note: Some children with autism are liable to categorize events simultaneously. Did baby sister cry because somebody was yelling? Or did somebody yell because baby sister was crying? This type of uncertainty may also characterize the early development of a non-autistic child. The non-autistic child is able to develop strategies early on for interpreting such incidents (through communication and affective attunement with adults). For children with autism, however, situations like these may indicate a sort of causality that is often inappropriate for dealing with emotional conflicts.

Social behaviour is governed not by causality, but by people's intentions. This can make people quite difficult to understand, so one would assume that a child would need far more time to develop competence within this social world. But early on the child understands people's intentions. Try to sneak a dummy away from the mouth of a six-month-old infant and see what happens. The infant will look up, not at the dummy nor the hand that took it. The child gazes directly into your eyes as if trying to read your intentions: What's up? Do we know each other? Are you smiling? Is it fun?

It becomes clear just how complex and how fundamental it is to be able to read and understand intentions when meeting a person who lacks this skill.

Says a young man with autism: 'I know that people communicate with each other through their eyes, but I cannot understand what they say.' Compared to this young man we live a life of luxury. We understand each other's body language and facial expressions immediately, and obtain free information just by looking at other people. We think in terms of intentions and social context – much in the same way that a musical person thinks in melody and rhythm. An autistic person has to memorize and understand every new social situation step by step.

A non-autistic child's experience of the world integrates cause–effect information as well as intention. For children with autism, the circumstances appear to be different.

The **physical** approach	The **social** approach
A 'chew on, shake, explore' world	A 'communicating with' world
Regularity	*Regularity*
Cause–effect	Intention
Activity	*Activity*
Exploring oneself through action (sensorimotor activity)	Exploring oneself through mirroring (sharing and attuning emotions)
Exploring behaviour (manipulating the object)	Playing behaviour (relating to the object)
Processing information	*Processing information*
Cognitive – perceptual	Emotional – empathetic
Concrete	Abstract – dynamic
The effect	*The effect*
Realization (understanding functions)	Experience (understanding context)

The child's immediate experience and organization of the world (from 0 to 9 months)

Children with autism often try to comprehend the social world by applying cause-and-effect logic. This is a demanding task.

We expect children to be able to read our moods easily and immediately understand our intentions. It is no wonder that serious communication difficulties tend to arise.

We may not even be aware of the problem, as we hardly ever have to pay conscious attention to this aspect of communication. We assume that children will understand what we mean and we are oblivious to our own habits and expectations which may become obstacles to our understanding of children with autism.

PROBLEM AREA 2
Communication and dialogue

By the age of about nine months, a series of qualitative changes occur in the infant's perception of her surroundings. At this age, the child normally knows that objects continue to exist although they may disappear from sight for a period of time. This reflects the baby's ability to form a representational image of objects (object permanence). It may sound complicated, but every parent perceives this transition.

When a child of six months throws her teddybear out of the pram, the toy is gone and forgotten. When a child of nine months throws her bear from the pram, she bursts into tears and cries until an adult picks up the toy again. One may barely have turned one's back, when the toy is thrown out again and so the game continues. At this age, 'peekaboo' games often become very popular with the child.

The development of the ability to form these sustained representations of objects is followed by the development of a series of new behavioural abilities in the child. The most essential of these is the baby's ability to share her experience of the world with an adult. The baby begins to point out and draw attention to things she finds exciting. She also learns to relate to adults in simple interchanges (joint attention).

This situation (which will be familiar to many readers) might occur when a visitor comes to the house.

The child of nine months:

1. Looks at mummy and, through body language and facial expression, gives clear indications of her own experience of the situation. (For example, I'm scared of this strange person.)

2. Perceives the mother's expression as an indication of the situation. (Don't be nervous – it's nice to have company.)

3. Attunes her own emotional experience with that of the mother.

4. Acts on this new information (the child accepts the stranger).

Note: Quite a lot of children with autism do not develop active spoken language. This may be caused by their lack of understanding of the possibilities of communication. It could also be due to their lower developmental level, or specific problems of a dysphasic nature.

Some children with autism develop spoken language, a comprehensive vocabulary, clear grammatical understanding, and so on. All children on the autistic spectrum have problems with dialogue and affective attunement (pragmatics).

We are talking about real dialogue, where both people give their interpretation of an incident (the stranger's arrival) and where two different sets of impressions are attuned – and result in common behaviour (the acceptance of the stranger).

Throughout their life people with autism will have major problems when talking about their experiences, and will find it very difficult attuning their emotional experiences with those of other people. Non-autistic children usually master this kind of dialogue during the first year of infancy – that is, long before they develop a spoken language.

Early dialogue (joint attention) precedes the development of imagination and fantasy. It is not surprising that social reciprocity, communication and imagination are all problems for children with autism. To understand the connection between these areas, we should try to imagine what a child's universe is like during the first eighteen months of her life.

PROBLEM AREA 3
Mental imaging and imagination

During early development, things are perceived by the child as they appear, not as they are. The child can see, smell, feel, taste and hear the world – a world which consists of more than what merely appears to the senses.

The child experiences the world through all her senses, yet still lacks an awareness that other people may have experiences that are different from her own. The internal representation of the world is transformed into a reconstruction which resembles whatever the child sees, hears, and so on. Thus the child is 'captured' by an external reality, which she may be able to register – but can rarely transform.

Many children with autism seem to maintain a concrete and literal (almost photographic) experience of the world throughout the course of their lives.

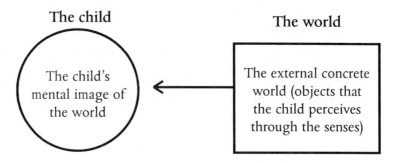

The child's first mental perception of the physical world.

When the non-autistic child is about nine months old, she is able to experience joint attention; her experience of the world begins to be attuned with that of the adult. As a result, the child's representational image changes considerably. The stranger by now is more than an unknown guest paying a visit – her arrival is also an event to be interpreted in the light of interaction with the adult. The child now has to relate to two representational images simultaneously: her own and that of the adult. One could say that representationally, the child shifts from 'mono' to 'stereo'.

Note: The representational images presented here primarily cover the physical perception of the world. The child may develop a similar model of her relationships with adults she is close to. Such a model should be dynamic and is primarily an emotional categorization of experiences. The process of integrating such representations into a coherent relational experience, is assumed to be very difficult for children with autism. A detailed review of the representational system is not given here. Interested readers should refer to Stern (1997) for a fascinating presentation of this model.

At this age, an event is no longer reduced to what one *sees, hears, tastes, smells* or *feels*, or whatever one may *know* about it in advance. An event becomes something which can be *interpreted* and *understood/realized*. Something one can imagine and act upon.

Early dialogue/joint attention, when a child compares her own feelings to those of others – and her own experience to that of the adult – is an important basis for the subsequent development of fantasy and imagination in the child.

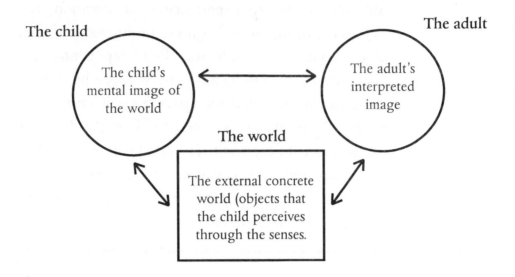

The child integrates his own and the adult's perceptions of the world.

The above figure illustrates how the child's mental image is complemented by the adult's interpretation. The child realizes that 'my image' is not the same as 'the other's image' and that 'my experience' is not the same as 'the other's experience'. The child needs to attune the two images, as well as her own and the other's emotional experience.

Such experiences and realizations are difficult for children with autism because of their problems understanding the social world.

When you close your eyes and recall your bedroom in your mind's eye, this is a representation – an internal copy. To a certain extent, children can make such representations from the age of nine months (object consistency) onwards. On the other hand, if you wanted to refurnish the living room, you would need a more flexible imagination.

From the onset of eighteen months, a non-autistic child is able to make flexible mental images; this indicates that she is able to imagine a world that is different from what she sees — one may refurnish, interpret, comment and give one's imagination free reign for new possibilities. The child can imagine a plastic toy to be alive, or that her teddybear has wet its pants.

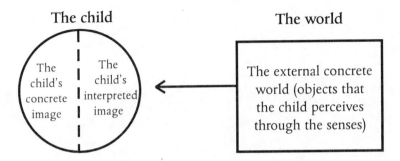

An illustration of the child's innate ability to create flexible images of the world.

As the illustration indicates, we are talking about images that are more internal: there is the 'concrete' world and then there are the many imaginary possibilities one has to modify this world.

Children with autism generally have major problems creating flexible images.

THE CHILD MAKES AN 'INTERNAL LIBRARY' OF DAILY ROUTINES (SCRIPTS)

Until now, we have referred to images as a collection of internal 'still' photos of the surrounding world, but this is obviously a simplification, because we (and the child) usually perceive the world in sequences: in short action and logical sequences.

From the age of six months, a non-autistic child is able to express expectations of short sequences of events. A child often stretches her arms, expecting to be picked up when an adult approaches. A hungry child reacts with joy and impatience as the sounds of cooking from the kitchen set off an inner sequence of images: cooker – table – plate – food from Mum.

Daily routines and family rituals are essential to a child's development, as rhythm, timing and events may be predicted. The toddler enjoys being in situations where she is able to guess 'what comes next'.

The child's first internal sequences of images may be quite rigid. Parents may be confronted with an inflexible response if they try to change the goodnight ritual of a two-year-old toddler. The child is *not* indifferent to the order in which she brushes her teeth, is read a story and sung a goodnight song. As she develops more flexible images, she becomes more skillful at foreseeing that a sequence of actions may be altered.

These initial internal images of well-known daily routines are called *scripts*. Scripts are like film scripts, outlining the sequences of a certain event (eg setting the table). Thus scripts form an inner working model of what usually occurs in a certain kind of situation.

Children with autism will have difficulty forming flexible scripts throughout their lives and tend to be dependent on events occurring in the same way every time.

Many children with autism have a clear conception of what a funfair is. If you ask the child to describe what a funfair is, she may start rattling off what you can do at a funfair: first you go through the entrance, then on to the roller coaster, then get an ice-cream, then a boat ride, and so on.

A chance or unexpected event may throw the child off this familiar and inflexible script. One mother explained how her son had started screaming and insisted that the family leave the funfair, just because they had used another entrance for a change. Only when the child was put on the roller coaster did he relax again.

Play is a way of making scripts of a child's daily routines – they become visual, accessible and concrete. Through play, we can demonstrate a variety of options for developing an established script (eg, that there is more than one entrance to the funfair), and at the same time can show respect for a child's need for the recognition and repetition of a familiar action sequence.

THE CHILD'S UNDERSTANDING OF THE INTENTIONAL BEHAVIOUR OF OTHER PEOPLE

The child's understanding of intention and goal-directed behaviour stems from social interaction.

The non-autistic child is born into a social world and has her first experiences through interacting with humans. The first five months of life are characterized by a close interchange of emotional signals between infant and adult. During this time, the child learns a lot about herself via mirroring – not in an ordinary mirror – it takes a few months before a child recognizes her own reflection in a mirror – but through those adults she is close to from birth.

A child between nine and twelve months of age is able to relate to humans and objects simultaneously. She shifts her attention between these two foci. This sort of interaction initiates an awareness of how humans and objects are interrelated.

During the course of the second year, the child gains an awareness of how people act intentionally. Humans direct their emotions and intentions towards the surrounding world. Early dialogue – joint attention – supports the child's comprehension of this connection. Two-year-olds have a pretty good idea of how, when people want to obtain certain objects, they act to get these objects, and how their emotions reflect whether they reach their goals or not.

At the age of about three, the child realizes that people act differently from one another and that they have different goals and needs. The three-year-old child is quite often very clever at keeping score of whom to ask for certain things. Is it Mum or Dad you should ask for an ice-cream?

The four-year-old takes this a step further. She can postpone asking Dad for an ice-cream until Mum has stepped outside. The four-year-old is aware of how people act according to the information they are given and that by withholding certain facts, you can give pleasure as well as cheat or manipulate.

The autistic child has great difficultly understanding how people act intentionally and how to pick out the meaningful elements of people's behaviour.

Autism as a condition is therefore closely associated with the concept of *meaning*. Where most children acknowledge the meaning and connections in life through analysis and intuition, children with autism are often left to guide themselves with only their sensory perception. They seldom have other options.

They often find themselves in situations they find hard to understand or predict – where they are overwhelmed with feelings and impressions they are unable to analyze – or where they get preoccupied with details or sensory impressions that seem irrelevant to most people.

Non-autistic people look for meaningful elements, or a common framework for understanding – they often pick up on something very easily from a small amount of information.

Children with autism constantly need to establish stable perceptual images and they find it difficult to see beyond the things they see or hear. Their behaviour, therefore, often appears to be 'echo-like' – with the same behaviour and ritual performed again and again.

Much attention has been given to their inability to make social contact; children with autism are often described as being closed, fearful and uninterested in social situations. It is important to comprehend the underlying causes of this problem.

Children with autism are rarely unaware of social contact, and quite a few even insist on it to a degree that seems remarkable – but this does not mean that they show the reciprocity and empathy which usually characterizes the social interaction of a child.

In the subsequent chapters, the authors describe play activities with a variety of objectives. The most important objective is to involve the child in a social context, which forms the natural platform for all play behaviour.

Many children with autism seem to be at a very early developmental stage in their play. They need to be approached at their own level. You need to create a framework and set the stage for play in a way that makes it both possible and attractive. This requires special attention to aspects such as visualization, imitation, mirroring, taking turns and being concrete and specific.

The characteristics
and patterns of play

WHAT IS PLAY?

How and why we play differs according to our point of reference. The social psychologist would possibly be interested in observing how the child prepares himself for the demands and roles of society through play. The psychoanalytical psychologist will place special value on the child's personality development and emotional attachment. The cognitively-oriented psychologist will pay attention specifically to the functional dimension of play and the value of the imagination, self-realization and the interpretation of other people's intentions.

No single perspective is the 'right' one – they all relate to different dimensions of play. For children with autism, it is natural to use a cognitive approach as it deals with some of the essential problems associated with autism (imagination, self-awareness, etc). This model cannot stand alone though as it has limited application to the emotional aspects of autism.

Play belongs to the social dimension which is often hard to explain in logical terms. Here are some features of non-autistic children's play:

- Children play regardless of cultural nationality.

- Children play solely for play's sake. The activity is an end in itself and is not intended to produce anything (in contrast to, say, carrying out a task).

- Play supports the child's social understanding: the roles and themes (scripts) which are acted out during play develop the child's insight into social rules and conventions.

- Play stems from the child's personal perception of reality.

- Play is a creative activity in that the child expresses and becomes more aware of himself through interaction with the world around him.

- Children mirror each other during play and thereby reinforce and develop their personal experiences.

- Play is a platform for imagination and fantasy where the child juggles with reality by pretending that certain events actually happen.

- Play provides the child with an opportunity for 'stepping back' and viewing a situation from the outside: 'Teddy bear needs food, just like myself' – or 'When the doll is me, what happens if it pushes its younger brother'?

- Play is based on voluntary activities and pleasure. The child plays out of choice and shows strong attention and absorption during play. Play is often accompanied with humming, sparkling eyes and other signs of enthusiasm and involvement.

- Play is the child's unique way of expressing himself.

EARLY FORMS OF PLAY

The child's first 'play object' is the adult. During initial interaction, the child and the adult communicate, play and experiment through facial expression, gestures, sounds, imitation and timing – and play activity is often accompanied with positive expressions like smiling, twitching and little squeals of delight.

The object's properties affect the child's play activities. In the early years, play with objects can be separated into the following four categories:

Sensorimotor play

Explorative play involves the child relating to one thing at a time (rolling, turning, spinning, sucking, throwing etc). The child, for instance, may tap an object on the floor or put it into his mouth while smiling. Sensorimotor play like this is dominant during the first six to eight months of age and occurs simultaneously with early interaction/joint attention, when the child relates to one adult at a time (the dyade).

Organizing play

In organizing play, toys are organized – with no attention given to their exact purpose. Toys may be put into a row, on top of each other, inside each other, and so on. This type of play occurs from six to nine months of age when the child has developed strategies for examining the surrounding world and begins to understand that objects have enduring qualities. At this age the child is also becoming aware of his own actions and those of other people. Imitation, where the child, for instance, copies the behaviour of other people or the use of objects without being aware of why he does it, can be viewed as a socially oriented variation of organizing play.

Functional play

Functional play dominates from the age of nine to twelve months and is accompanied with the sharing behaviour of joint attention (early dialogue). Play items at this age are used intentionally, according to their function. The child is aware that other people give their attention to objects and is preoccupied with imitating the object-oriented behaviour of other people.

Pretend play

The child usually makes use of pretend play from the age of about eighteen months. The child may pretend that a block is a car (object replacement), that teddy bear is alive (projection of pretended qualities) or there is a lion underneath the bed (pretended existence). Pretend play is a valuable opening to the emotional and cognitive universe of the child. It reflects the child's ability to form internal representations (the ability to imagine what other people are thinking).

The following four incidents illustrate a non-autistic child's spontaneous use of a play object at different levels of development:

1. Lukas at five months of age puts the TV remote control in his mouth, and then he knocks it onto the floor while squealing with delight.

2. Lukas at eight months of age sits with the remote control, while pointing at everybody and everything. He still is unaware of its function, but he has seen his older siblings fight for the right to use this important object.

3. Lukas at nine months of age finds the red button on the remote control in the middle of his elder sister's favourite program. He points towards the TV — pushes — and squeals happily. Lukas is now able to play functionally.

4. Lukas at twenty-two months of age runs around with the remote control – sometimes he holds it to his ear, says 'loh' – and pretends he is speaking on a mobile phone.

The above examples show the possible development of a non-autistic child. It must be stressed that these are typical developments, and do not reflect actual situations. Not all non-autistic children play in clearly defined ways. Moreover, the four phases can easily be present at the same time in the child.

OBSERVATIONS OF PLAY AMONG CHILDREN WITH AUTISM

Although a number of children with autism are able to make use of sensorimotor, organizational and functional play during a test situation, and even though some of them with support are able to engage in pretend play, a child with autism will rarely be perceived as a playing child.

Children with autism often make use of objects in such an inflexible stereotypical way that they miss out considerably on experiences with simple manipulation and combination that other children gain during the first few years of life. Functional play is not used as often or as spontaneously as with non-autistic children. The pattern of play is often described as being mechanical, lacking the natural tendency to explore, with individual activities seeming isolated from any context. Pretend play is rare and when it does occur, it is usually dominated by certain themes, associated either with special interests or specific TV programs that the child is preoccupied with and imitates. Many studies have focused on the development of play among children with autism. We would like to concentrate on three of the most important studies.

The first systematic description of the autistic syndrome was given by Leo Kanner in 1943. In this presentation, Kanner emphasized the limited ability for play which characterizes people with autism.

Another great pioneer in the field of autism is Lorna Wing. During the 1970s she carried out a series of fundamental research projects, and in 1979 together with Judith Gould, she demonstrated how only very few children with autism use symbolic play. In their studies the few who showed signs of symbolic play, played in a very stereotypical manner, which was indifferent to other children's suggestions. A pilot group of children with developmental disabilities, but not autism, showed spontaneous and varied symbolic play according to their developmental age.

In 1985, Simon Baron-Cohen, Alan Leslie and Uta Frith introduced the so-called 'Theory of Mind' hypothesis and autism-related research was intensified as a result of this new opening.

One of the fundamental elements of their hypothesis was the link between a child's ability to pretend play and his potential ability to understand his own behaviour as well as other people's. It became essential, therefore, to establish whether the lack of pretend play among children with autism was caused by a lack of motivation to enter into this form of play, or by an inability to form images.

Such clarification requires an exact differentiation between functional play and pretend play. According to Alan Leslie's theory, the ability to pretend is recognized as a deliberate disregard for reality, where the child is simultaneously aware of a real situation and creates an image of it as being something else. As an example of the differentiation between functional play and pretend play, one may refer to a child playing with her doll's set. If the child holds the cup to her mouth and says 'ah!', we may talk of functional play. All the child needs to do is to imitate what other people do with the same cups – this does not require imagination. If the child, on the other hand, imagines she is a princess throwing a tea party, this may be called pretend play because reality is ignored.

The conflict between the motivational hypothesis (that children do not make use of pretend play because of lack of emotional involvement) and the competence hypothesis (that children do not make use of pretend play because of an inability to form images), reflects a crucial dilemma in autism research: Does autism have an emotional or a cognitive origin?

In support of the *motivational hypothesis*, one finds that children with autism do poorly in spontaneous and free play situations, whilst in a test situation they function at a much higher level, if they are offered a reward and if the adult structures play (ie when play is externally motivated).

In support of the *competence hypothesis*, one finds that autism reduces the functioning level specifically at the (higher level) function of imagination. Many children with autism may handle an object as if it were something else (a stick is used as a cigar) and handle a doll as if it were alive (let it walk, eat, sleep etc.), but they cannot pretend that they have a different experience of the world which is considerably distinct from their own. They are incapable of attributing an actual mental life with its own wishes and imagination to the doll.

Both hypotheses stem from a clear perception of autism as an organically caused problem.

We would argue that there are cognitive aspects as well as emotional ones underlying the absence of pretend play and in the first part of the book we have argued for a close connection between the emotional, social and cognitive developmental aspects.

In the next part we will describe how this theory can be applied to an educational praxis and share what we have learnt about how children with autism interact.

PART 2

Preparation of
a play sequence

The infant has innate patterns of attention and response which allow her to interact with the primary attachment figure. The non-autistic child explores, is curious and is in constant and dynamic dialogue with her environment. The non-autistic child is born into a social world.

Children with autism typically have a far more difficult start in life. They do not have a non-autistic child's immediate understanding of the connection between her own actions and those of other people, nor an awareness of the intentions underlying human behaviour.

If we refer back to the table on page 28, we can see how the distinction between 'the material/physical world' and 'the social world' can help us to understand aspects of autism.

Only some children with autism are capable of dealing with the logical sequence of actions which characterize the physical level. When you want to create a learning environment through socio-educational activities, this may be compensated for by establishing a 'learning disability friendly environment', where structure, rules and predictability (causality) are prioritized and where visualization and perception are highly valued. Among new initiatives that incorporate this educational framework, the learning strategies inspired by TEACCH (Treatment and Education for Autistic and related Communication-handicapped Children) should be mentioned, as well as the so-called 'Social Stories' (Carol Gray, 1995).

Strategies designed to compensate for the disability should be central when preparing any form of educational or treatment intervention for children with autism. They cannot stand alone, however. There is a need for other strategies to enable personal development at a social level. Is it possible to develop such strategies?

To understand social contexts you need to participate in them. For instance, you learn about love by being involved in a loving relationship and about friendship by experiencing friendship. Among other reasons, this is why our knowledge of love and friendship is as diverse as it is.

For many people with autism, the goal of having a friend or a girl/boyfriend is unobtainable, and even the experience of connectedness with another person can be associated with great difficulties.

We have emphasized the non-autistic child's innate awareness of the connection between her own actions and those of other people as a key to social, communicative and representational development.

Two children with autism are never alike, and the symptoms they show change according to the rhythm of the their development. Difficulties associated with the experience of connectedness, however, will always be dominant within the autistic syndrome.

In normal development, adult caregivers represent the first play objects for the child and when the child first begins to play, this is manifested in exchanges of emotions and gestures with the caregivers (mirroring).

In test situations, many children with autism have specific problems associated with imitation and mirroring. This is therefore an important area to focus on.

Play involves an interaction between two or more people. We need to link play activity with an experience of connectedness – a connection which a non-autistic child understands intuitively, but which children with autism often have great difficulty experiencing.

The framework we will outline has been adapted to the developmental potential of each individual child. In this way, the child herself will determine the level at which play should be carried out.

Play can easily start as an interaction between one child and one adult, but it is essential to give children who are sufficiently resourceful the opportunity to play together with other children.

Note: Mirroring is defined as the immediate and biological ability to pick up on and participate in communication based on imitation. Here we talk of an amodal way of perceiving, where perception and self-awareness interact. In early development, mirroring represents an essential step towards affective attunement with the primary adult.

The task is simply about: making it fun and attractive to be together with other people, while being aware that it is not all that easy. It demands a great deal of consideration on behalf of the adult to arrange situations the children will find amusing and where they will be motivated to interact.

THE RATIONALE FOR THE PLAY STRATEGIES

The following discussion of play sequences attempts to keep two perspectives in mind: that children with autism are just like other children, and yet different from all other children. The play sequences are inspired by the pattern of a typical child's development, as well as adapted to the individual child's special development.

The play strategies will focus on the following themes:

- attention, expectation and shared focus
- imitation and mirroring
- parallel play and play dialogue
- script and social stories
- shifts in taking turns
- games and rules in playing.

Setting the stage and visualization can further develop the child's social and instrumental competencies.

CHOICE OF PLAY MATERIALS

The toy is a working tool which should be chosen with the same care with which an experienced craftsman would choose his tools. Toys should be recognizable and easy to handle. If the child is presented with too many toys at the same time it may be confusing. Toys should be appealing but not to the extent where the child loses interest in other things. So it is a matter of finding the right balance when choosing toys!

Toys which rely considerably on a causal effect are often good for motivating children (ie, soap gun, spinning wheel with light and sound, a balloon car that drives when the balloon is inflated).

Doll's houses and other miniature objects are also recommended as they are suitable for visualizing and specifying daily routines (described in individual play sequences).

SETTING THE STAGE

For non-autistic children, the predominant elements of play are contact and exploration. For children with autism, you often have to prepare and monitor the child's environment to ensure that contact and exploration will be attractive to the child. Therefore, setting the stage is important.

Setting the stage literally means to mark out the 'stage' where play activities take place. The child should be ensured the optimal conditions for playing an active role. Thus the adult acts as a stage director providing the child with the necessary support.

A table can be an ideal framework as the top of the table has a distinct outline. When two individuals play together it may be appropriate at first for each person to be given a table as their domain or to divide the table (eg with coloured tape) so each person gets a section. An equivalent division can be used even if play occurs in other places (eg on the floor).

The play material is then introduced and the rules are explicitly illustrated with or without words. This simple introduction to the situation helps the child to understand the intention of the play activity, as the stage will be the foundation for play. Children's direct comprehension of visually clear directions helps them to become less dependent on the adult.

Playing is a way of being together which gradually becomes an integrated part of daily activities. The stage can be expanded, creative or sensorimotor activities can be introduced, or the stage can be taken outside. This part of setting the stage is not addressed in this book.

The crucial point is to guide the child – not to control her.

Examples of play sequences

ATTENTION, EXPECTATIONS AND SHARED FOCUS

F or children with autism, it is difficult to share experiences and expectations with other people. Attention, expectations and shared focus are fundamental to play activities, to enhance the attention skills of children at an early developmental level.

Setting the stage and choice of play material

A table is outlined as the stage and the child sits opposite the adult. The toys are introduced one by one, from a colourful box where they have been stored.

By first hiding the toy in the box you ensure that:

- The child's attention is drawn towards the box as well as to the person who presents it – thus the social element of play is made obvious.

- The child and the adult have distinct roles in a shared sequence of actions.

- The child's attention, curiosity and expectations are increased by integrating several senses – the colour of the box, the sound of the contents when the box is shaken, etc.

- The child has time to adjust before having to act and respond.

- The adult has the chance to increase interaction by using timing (when the child's impatience and expectations are timed, the toy may be handed over as soon as an appropriate level of motivation has been reached).

- Repeating a social routine that becomes automatic gives the child the opportunity to invent novel activities (putting new objects in the box, reversing the roles, so the child hands the box to the adult or another child, etc).

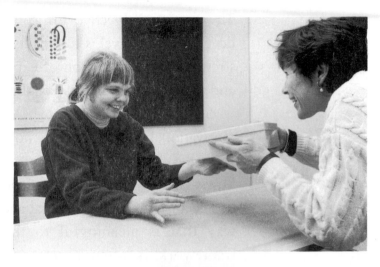

An attractive box may encourage interaction. The child's attention is drawn towards the box and at the same time the child's curiosity is aroused – what's hidden in the box?

Curiosity may lead the child actively to examine the contents of the box.

There's a clear reason for the adult to be involved helping out.

The primary objective for children at a very early developmental level is to establish simple routines that strengthen the formation of expectations, recognition and social interaction between the child and the adult.

Social contact and interaction are the primary motivational factors for the non-autistic child at an early developmental level. For children with autism, however, motivation is often dependent on our ability to select exciting play material and to present play in a way that is meaningful to the child. A planned framework is often necessary for setting up the interaction.

Shared focus – the spinning top.

THE PLAY THEME

The theme and content of play can be gradually developed using the child's own stock of experience.

Simple, familiar events or routines (scripts), that will evoke recognition and motivation are suitable themes for play. For example, a 'morning routine' (when the doll gets up, goes to the bathroom, brushes her teeth), a cookery lesson at school, a visit to the swimming pool, a meal at McDonald's, a birthday party, a telephone call, a trip to the funfair.

The script is developed in a concrete way by the use of appropriate toys and additional visual aids and pictures, if required.

When the child is competent enough to play with another child, the adult should take on a less intrusive role, but be continually supportive when needed.

In our experience, the adult often prevents social interaction between children because they automatically relate to the adult instead of to one another.

IMITATION AND MIRRORING

At six months of age, the non-autistic child is already aware that his actions can be imitated by other people. Some children with autism have difficulties realizing the connection between their own behaviour and that of other people until later, at school age.

Through play, it is possible to make the connection between the adult's behaviour and that of the child more obvious and concrete.

To set the stage and choice of play material:

- Throughout the actual play sequence, the child is introduced to just a few objects at a time.

- At the outset, the play objects are divided into two similar sets: One in front of the child and one which is only accessible to the adult (perhaps hidden from the child for a surprise effect).

- The child has plenty of time to choose his toy and then the adult takes an identical toy and imitates the child's actions.

- The adult then takes the lead, attempting to make the child imitate her actions.

The selection of two identical sets of toys has many advantages:

- Completely identical objects inspire attention, motivation and wonder.

- It is possible clearly to imitate the child's actions.

- The child experiences how his taking the initiative can direct the adult's actions.

- Joint and simultaneous actions reinforce the child's own initiative.

- The adult is able to guide instead of taking over.

It often makes children happy and motivated when an adult 'overacts' during play – this clearly indicates that the child's behaviour is dependent on that of the adult. Toys should be big and conspicuous at the beginning for this exaggeration to be achieved.

Note: The non-autistic child has an intuitive understanding of the connection between his own behaviour and that of others. Such an understanding would be difficult for many children with autism to obtain.

The interdependence of the child's behaviour and that of the adult is drawn out by the choice of big and identical toy objects.

Teenage play

It is crucial for play themes and content to be both motivating and appropriate for each age group.

The theme

The theme in the following example is a simple imitation game selected from the young girl's sphere of interest.

Teenage girls often like playing at being women and dressing up with hats and lipstick, and so on.

The stage

The participants sit opposite each other so the adult can act as a mirror for the young girl. The mirroring and sense of connectedness between the two players is reinforced by the use of two big, identical hats.

The table is divided with coloured tape to provide each participant with their own space and their own things.

The play materials

Objects from the make-up bag – in two sets.

The play sequence

At first the adult directs and the girl imitates. Every initiative from the girl is accepted and reinforced. Gradually the stage is set for role reversal to allow the girl to take the initiative. Play can be developed further using themes such as 'the dressing table', 'the hairdresser' etc – but the emphasis is on play, not teaching! After some time, a girl of the same age or maybe a sibling can take the place of the adult. It is essential for the adult to use her body language and facial expressions to show that playing should be fun.

Imitation play can be developed further by adding a few effects, so they become motivating elements for teenagers. Here a sense of connectedness is established using two large, identical hats.

Parallel play

The following is a description of three examples of play sequences, where the principles of imitation and mirroring are developed further into parallel play.

At the age of about eighteen months the non-autistic child starts to use parallel play. In terms of normal development, parallel play is a phase where the child is still not able to engage in actual play dialogue with children of the same age. Nevertheless he is obviously interested in his peers and plays near other children, which is an indication of the desire to establish social contact.

By focusing on parallel play in the construction of simple play sequences, social interaction is established.

The stage may be a table, divided by coloured tape (or two narrow tables put together). The participants – first one child with an adult – face each other from opposite sides of the table; this sets the stage. The division provides the child with the required 'personal space', as he is able to ignore direct social demands from the adult. At the same time, the child is able to approach his partner when he wants to.

Children with autism have difficulties in identifying meaningful social activity. Often one observes how these children attempt to copy play sequences and make them identical each time. A demand or suggestion by the adult can invoke anxiety and confuse the child. A child with autism may perceive the most insignificant change as a major change which causes the inner script of the play to disintegrate.

Through parallel play, it is possible to develop the child's playing pattern further, as the adult just mirrors

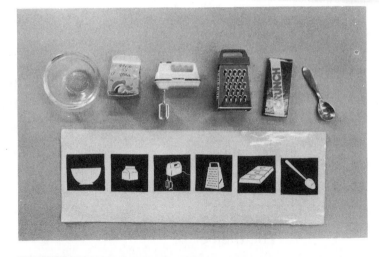

Play with cooking utensils.

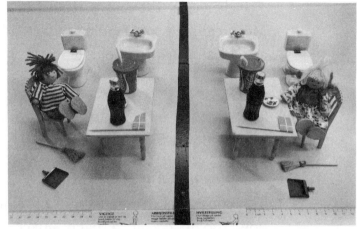

Parallel play where two children can play together.

Play with visual scripts.

the child's play sequence, while simultaneously providing new ideas.

When the child's private sphere is respected, he is able to concentrate his excess energy on imitating behaviour, and in this way to develop his playing pattern without becoming frustrated by complex demands.

Playing at cooking

The theme
The theme in this case is related to school activities. Most children are familiar with and very fond of activities related to cooking.

The stage
The stage is a table which is divided in two by a line marked down the middle.

The play materials
This consists of two similar sets of miniature objects: a bowl, some cream, a hand mixer, a grater, some chocolate, a spoon; as well as a series of pictograms of the objects used. The toys are simple, quite neutral and easy to recognize and therefore are not distracting to the child.

The play sequence
The child realizes that the adult has exactly the same set of toys. The child immediately recognizes the theme and begins to match the objects with the pictograms. As this routine is a familiar and therefore not a demanding task, the child can also check to see whether the adult is copying his actions at the same time. The child may stop

The child recognizes the cooking theme. He checks on the adult to see if she is copying his actions.

And the other way round – now it is the adult who leads. The toys act as source of motivation and focus for the child and adult when they interact.

at this point and the adult can take over and grate 'the chocolate' into the bowl, for example. The child copies the adult, then may start to mix with the spoon which is in turn imitated by the adult. Play activities continue – it may be agreed that the adult leads at first and the child imitates, and then the roles are reversed. The toys become in this way a source of motivation and focus for both participants.

One of the miniature sets can be exchanged with real objects, giving the child a more realistic idea of the consequences of what he is doing. One of our children suggested (by turning his miniature bowl upside down) that the adult should do the same with her bowl, and it was full of real whipped cream!

The objective

The objective of this constructed play sequence is to help children with the transition from simple imitation play to a set-up where toys are combined with well-known scripts and the situation is therefore more complex. When the adult guides without taking over, the child is open to interaction. This play model can be used with varying content.

Playing with dolls

The theme

Many children (both boys and girls) like to play with dolls, but may lack the initiative and ideas for getting started. We chose a well-known doll's game as the theme.

The stage

The stage is a table which is divided in two by a line marked down the middle.

The play materials

Toys such a dolls, dolls' tea sets and toiletries are familiar to children. This helps children to think of ordinary and well-known activities: feeding the doll, giving it something to drink, combing its hair, letting it use the potty, giving it a bath and so on.

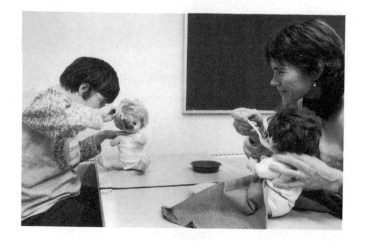

The doll's birthday. A familiar and motivating event related to the child's own experiences is often an ideal way to start play and interaction.

The play sequence

The sequence allows the child to play by monitoring and imitating the adult. The child's own initiative is immediately reinforced by the adult's imitation.

Parallel play when two children play together

The theme

The theme is an extended version of doll's play with daily activities.

The stage

The stage supports both children when they play together without further instructions from the adult.

The play materials

These are two similar sets of toys containing a doll, a table, a chair, a bottle of coke, a plate, a flag pole or balloon, a toilet, a sink, a broom and a dustpan.

The play sequence

First the children organize their own doll's toys. Then one child starts to play with his playmate's toys.

The dolls may pay visits to each other, and the balloon or flag may give them the idea of having a birthday party. The tables are set with plates and coke and cake. Then 'happy birthday' is sung. Afterwards the dishes must be washed and ...

The fact that the children got started at once came as a surprise. We were pleased to see the children keeping the game flowing and initiating new ideas.

*Each child organizes
his doll's toys in his
own marked area.*

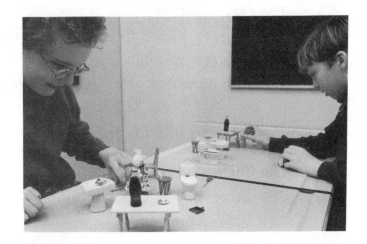

*'What a good idea to
pay a visit.'*

*'Let's play
together.'*

Comments

Right from the beginning, the children experienced a shared focus of attention and shared happiness while playing together. The form (the stage) and the content (the toys) provided the children with a framework for their games, which they would not have been able to establish themselves. This provided a framework for mutual inclusion while playing, without losing the basic aim in the process. The toys provided appropriate cues for the sequence (theme).

The children are able to support each other. In this case, the boy shows more initiative as well as being more vivacious. The girl is calmer as well as a little passive. Through mutual interaction, the children can increase their energy level, as well as calming down.

PLAY WITH VISUAL SCRIPTS

The stage

This consists of a table with no dividing line. The adult sits opposite the child. It is up to the child whether he would like to invite the adult to play or not.

The play materials

These consist of a story sequence in pictures with the corresponding toys. The picture story (the theme) illustrates a simple activity with two children on a picnic.

A sequence picture story may be the basis and inspiration of play. The child is given a subject for the story that can be developed further over time.

The play sequence

The play materials lead the children to match the toys with the corresponding pictures – a routine recognized from previous activities. On this occasion, the child immediately offers the adult one of the dolls. The story is enacted in the 'right' sequence, accompanied by spontaneous remarks that also refer to the adult's doll.

The objective

The objective of using a sequence story is to provide the child with a framework to outline and inspire play activities. The child is given a subject to play with. Many children with autism would play, but find it hard to invent the content of play. We know that children are supported by visual models in their accomplishment of daily tasks (work tasks, PE, cooking, etc). Children enjoy playing with sequence stories as 'how to play out the story' is made clear.

Comments

Be aware of the possible pitfall that the sequence story may inhibit the child's own initiative, because the choice of play becomes 'tied' to the illustrations. By adding some toys that are not linked directly to the story (eg an ambulance), the child is encouraged to add his own 'inventions' to the story.

As the focus is on play activity and not teaching, it is not important for the child to put the pictures in the right order or name the pictures etc. Demands for accurate language use by the child should also be avoided during play.

SOCIAL STORIES AS VISUAL SCRIPTS

People with autism have a reduced ability to read the rules of social interactions. These rules are often known as the 'unwritten social rules' (for how to behave) that non-autistic people acquire through interaction with other people (the social dimension). An example of a social convention is greeting other people. Where, when, how? Whom do you greet, and for how long?

Social stories, developed by Carol Gray in 1995, are short stories which describe a child in a given social situation, and outline the usual reactions connected to the situation.

Social stories may provide the child with a foothold in a social situation and a format for knowing how to behave in the situation. Using visual aids, social stories present the child with a series of actions by translating the logic of the social world into the logic of cause and effect. Social stories thus make the implicit, unwritten rules explicit.

Social stories as visual scripts may outline play activities much in the same manner as play with sequence picture stories. The child is able to act out the content in the social story with appropriate toys. Furthermore, in social stories the child is the main character, which usually increases his interest and motivation.

Play activities help to make the social aspects of the story more specific and concrete in a fun and comprehensible way. The script allows the child to enact the story several times, deepening his social understanding.

John and Peter play together

Sometimes John takes Peter's toy

Peter may call his Mum

Mum explains that the toy belongs to Peter

Social stories provide a framework for playing with dolls and other kinds of toys.

In Simon's home there is a VCR.

The VCR belongs to Mum and Dad.

Sometimes Mum and Dad forget to eject the videotape.

**When Simon discovers the videotape in the VCR
he may call for his Mum or Dad.**

Either Mum or Dad ejects the videotape from the VCR.

The starting point for social stories is an activity that concerns the child, or his environment. This increases his motivation for dealing with the issue – even through play.

Play with social stories is almost like teaching, because the content is determined by whatever we want to teach the child. This seems to go against the basic rule that play activities should not involve teaching.

It is still recommended that social stories are included in play activities. The stories may illustrate the social dimension in a concrete way, and the child is presented with a stage inviting him to be the main actor – a role which often poses great difficulties for children with autism.

PLAY WITH TAKING TURNS
Your turn – my turn

When you play it is essential that you are able to take turns. This means knowing when to take turns in the activity and being aware that each player should have his own turn.

As described previously, the non-autistic child is brought up with this type of turn-taking from early dialogue with his mother/father.

The child with autism does not naturally take turns when he interacts and needs help to learn how to. Most children are able to learn the rules for taking turns easily, if the rules are made specific through the use of examples.

We have used a cap to mark who's turn it is. When a turn is over, the cap is passed on to the next person in line. In this way, the cap indicates whose turn it is right now, as well as whose turn it will be next, by the cap being passed to the next person. The cap helps to keep the focus on the player and therefore simplifies the interaction for the others.

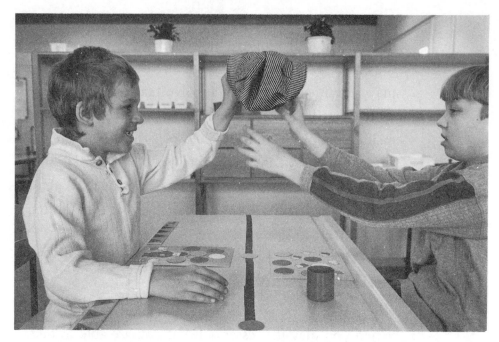

When the rules are kept straightforward, the child has enough spare energy to experience the social dimension, through happiness, excitement, expectation —

— and impatience, 'It's my turn now!'

The child sees his actions reflected in what his playmates are doing, and this visual reflection helps him become more aware of his own actions.

Building a tower of blocks together

The play materials

The play materials are a set of coloured blocks.

The stage

The stage is a table that is marked with a line down the middle, just like in parallel play. The children sit opposite each other. A block, placed in the middle, is the beginning of the tower. The remaining blocks are placed on the dividing line.

The play sequence

The child with the cap (the agent) takes a block and puts it on top of the starter block. Then the cap is passed on to his playmate, who takes a new block and places it on top of the tower, and so on.

The taller the tower gets, the more the children's mutual attention increases, as it demands concentration and cooperation to get the tower as tall as possible. And when it eventually tumbles down everybody shouts with joy.

The clear structure of the play and the roles help the children to play together without an adult. This sharpens their mutual attention. The activity has a natural climax (when the tower tumbles down), which provides the play with tempo and flow.

Note: The term 'flow' applies to the climax ('the rush'), which builds up during non-autistic children's play.

The set-up is clear: The boy with the cap can take a block from the dividing line and put it on top of the tower.

The roles are reversed.

The taller the tower gets, the more the children's mutual attention increases, as it demands concentration and cooperation to get the tower as tall as possible. This reinforces the sensation of connectedness in the children – in working on something meaningful together.

The children's sense of connectedness is reinforced – they are working out something meaningful together.

The drama enacted by the children has many emotional dimensions, which come across clearly in the photographs.

The children express happiness, excitement, anticipation and impatience, and they watch their playmate expressing the same emotions as the roles are constantly reversed.

In this type of play sequence, it is possible to practise mirroring each other. The children gain important social experiences as well as possible self-insight.

GAMES AND GAME RULES
The coloured die game

The play materials
Two boards with pictures of coloured balloons, matching coloured discs and a coloured die. The die is rolled and the six balloons on the board are covered with the appropriate coloured discs. The first player to cover all his balloons correctly wins.

The stage and the play sequence
A table divided with a line marked down the middle. The children sit opposite one another, each with their board with coloured balloons. The discs are placed on the line in the centre. The player throwing the die wears the cap. After throwing the die, he picks up the coloured piece which matches the die throw. He passes the die and cup onto the next player who throws the die, and on it goes.

The coloured die indicates which colour disc you may take from the central line.

Although it is not your turn you can still help out.

Shared interest.

Most children find it easy to understand the rules of the game, though when two playmates play together without adult supervision the game often fails because of problems with social interaction. Accompanied by an adult they can easily play more complex games.

Experience shows that it is helpful for the children to clearly delineate the taking of turns, as a guide to stay on track, even if unforeseen things happen. Again the children gain a positive sense of self-worth while experiencing the fun of being together without the presence of adults.

GROUP PLAY

A group of children and adults engage in play activity together. The person who wears the red cap is in charge of the rules and materials (at first this is an adult and then a child). The person who's turn it is, the active player, wears the striped cap, plays and then passes on the cap to the next player.

The 'drawing cards' game

The stage, the theme and the play materials

The children sit around a table with the adult. The person with the red cap holds five cards in her hand without showing them to the other players. Three cards are marked with a picture (eg of a biscuit, chips or some candy) and two jokers are left blank. The person with the striped cap draws a card and the excitement mounts — what will the card be? Maybe the card is blank and you won't get anything!

The game has five cards, three cards are marked with different kinds of food and two cards are left blank. If you draw a blank card you don't get anything!

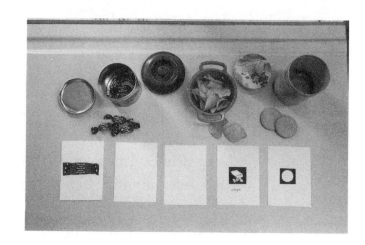

In group play two different caps are used: This helps the children to focus on the rules of the game (and the interaction).

The excitement increases mutual motivation and attention.

Comments

The participants find the rules easy to understand, which may make it easier for them to cope if a blank card is drawn. If a blank card is drawn, the player may look forward to the next turn for a better result.

This game is very popular. When you draw a card, you may get something to eat and this increases the excitement for the child whose turn it is. Most children have a good time (laughing out loud), when somebody draws a blank card. Other children are ready to cry when they draw one. Both reactions are emotional indicators of involvement. The drama that takes place during the game, allows the children to experience an important shared experience (the social dimension).

The play activity exemplifies how well these children cope with the use of rules, when they are comprehensible. For instance, the organizing child with the red cap passes the sweets to the player with the striped cap, instead of eating them herself.

'Choosing the toys' game

The stage, the theme and the toys

The children sit around a table with the adult. The organizer, at first an adult and then a child, with the red cap has a 'choosing cloth' with three different images of toys as well as a box with the corresponding toys.

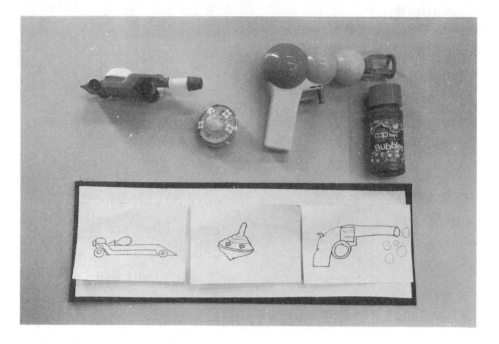

The play materials.

The play sequence and objectives

The organizer with the red cap asks the player with the striped cap: 'What would you like to try?' and/or pushes the cloth towards this person. The player with the striped cap says what she would like or points at the cloth and then passes the cloth with the chosen toy to the organizer with the red cap, who exchanges the cloth for the preferred toy. The player plays with the toy, while the other children watch (shared focus). The organizer decides when the turn is over by asking for the toy (verbally and/or by reaching out with her hand) and the striped cap is passed on to the next player who waits for her turn.

The objective of this play activity is to give the children a system and help them understand how they can use the toys when they play together.

The acting person with the striped cap chooses a toy from the pictures.

The organizer with the red cap exchanges the chosen picture with the toy.

You play with the toy – and the other children watch. When the children are sure of how they and the other children can play, it becomes easier and more fun to be a part of the interaction.

Comments

This kind of play activity is based on reciprocity (with or without the use of spoken language), that is:

- addressing someone else with an issue

- being able to receive a message and make a choice

- being able to receive a message and respond to it.

This kind of play activity may appear simple, but contains a series of tasks which are difficult for children with autism.

The visual rules help the children to include each other. Without visual aids, the children find this kind of play difficult and may become frustrated by it.

The dual demands

Most play activities demand both social skills and practical playing skills. Non-autistic people rarely perceive the social requirements as a strain, while children with autism experience them as the most difficult part of a task.

When you present a child with two difficult tasks at once, great care should be taken.

Example

A group of children are engaged in a play activity around a table and part of the objective is that every child gets a piece of candy. A jar with candy is passed around and the task – which may appear simple – makes a series of demands on each child:

- to keep one's attention on the jar
- to receive the jar from someone else
- to choose a piece of candy
- to name the particular candy
- to pick up the chosen candy
- to pass on the jar to the next child.

Most children would find this situation very easy to handle, but for children with autism the combination of both social and verbal demands may be confusing and the task may be too difficult.

When complex social demands are made of children, the content of play activities should be kept simple — and likewise when the practical content is more complex, the social demands should be smaller.

Some of the children in the project would initiate simple role plays when interacting with an adult. They sometimes set the stage for play with extended and dramatic content, delegated different roles to the adult and themselves, and acted with different voices, and so on. Their play, however, lacked reciprocity and there was no room for the adult's suggestions — the play would become a monologue, that only worked as long as the adult did not pressurize the child with social demands.

If these children are to *play together with* other children, the social context entails considerable demands, so the game chosen should be kept quite simple and preferably familiar.

Pressures or demands that inhibit the child should be avoided when he plays — play should be play and not teaching.

Summary and conclusion

Setting the stage for each of the play sequences provides the child with an opportunity to experience himself as part of an interaction.

While children experience parallel play activities and turn-taking, they are sharing and reflecting mutual actions and emotions.

We have argued for a close connection between emotional, social and cognitive aspects of development. The children's involvement in the prepared play sequences and the improved quality of their interaction following the play activities, supports the hypothesis for such a connection.

We have presented ideas which provide children, and the adults playing with them, with new choices for play activities. These choices are one method of preparing daily play activities in a structured way, that enhances and supports the play environment of children with autism.

Children with autism find it difficult to play in a spontaneous and varied way, but they can benefit from play activities if an environment is established to meet their needs.

We have demonstrated how to create such an environment, where children with autism, regardless of their developmental level, can partake in play activities. We hope that this book will be an inspiration for others to develop these children's potential for play.

Questionnaire for play observation

To gain an idea of a child's developmental level, it is useful to observe the child when he plays in free play situations as well as in prepared play situations with an adult.

1. FREE PLAY

A variety of play material is put on the floor before the child enters the room. The child is given enough time to get started, while the adult stays neutral and waits for the child to take the initiative spontaneously. *The play material should comprise*:

(a) Simple sensorimotor toys like blocks, soundmakers, etc

(b) Toys based on causality, which when activated release an effect, ie a car which makes a sound upon touch, a mechanical animal that must be wound up, a top, etc

(c) Functional toys like cars, dolls, doll's things, animals.

Carefully observe the child's behaviour and pay close attention to the following:

Choice of play material   YES   NO

1. Does the child choose a specific toy?   ☐   ☐

2. Does the child choose a specific *type* of toy?   ☐   ☐

3. No choice of toy.   ☐   ☐

4. Other.   ☐   ☐

Social behaviour during free play

	YES	NO
1. Does the child stay away from the adult?	☐	☐
2. Does the child involve the adult?	☐	☐
if yes, how:	☐	☐
(a) Does the child give or show the toy to the adult?	☐	☐
(b) Does the child ask for help?	☐	☐
(c) Instrumentally – does the child make use of the adult as an instrument?	☐	☐
(d) Other.	☐	☐

Play mode during free play

	YES	NO
1. Sensorimotor orientated, manipulative (chewing, sucking, throwing).	☐	☐
2. Organizing (putting blocks on top of each other, putting things in a box, etc).	☐	☐
3. Functional use of toy (driving a car, drinking from a doll's cup, combing the dolls hair, etc).	☐	☐
4. Imaginary/pretend play (pretend that the block is a car, the doll has human characteristics, etc).	☐	☐

2. SOCIAL INITIATIVE TAKEN BY THE ADULT

After a period of free play, the adult takes the initiative to play with the child.

Prepare short play sequences, which stimulate the child's curiosity (eg blow soap bubbles, wind a mechanical animal up, etc) and pay attention especially to the following:

	YES	NO
1. Does the child follow the adult's gaze towards an object out of reach?	☐	☐

2. Does the child ask the adult for the following:

(a) Help? ☐ ☐

(b) To repeat an amusing activity? ☐ ☐

(c) Objects out of reach? ☐ ☐

(d) Other? ☐ ☐

3. IMITATION

Imitate the child's behaviour (eg pat the table), and wait for the reaction.

	YES	NO
1. Does the child realize he is being imitated and does he want to continue?	☐	☐
2. Does the child attempt to imitate the adult?	☐	☐

4. SOCIAL ROUTINES AND EXPECTATION

	YES	NO
1. Does the child understand simple social routines (playing 'peekaboo', 'I'm coming to get you', tickling and so on) and does the child expect the adult to continue such games?	☐	☐

5. TAKING TURNS

	YES	NO
Is the child able to let an object go and take it back in a to and fro fashion (eg roll a ball, drive a car back and forth, play drums where the child and adult take turns hitting the drums)?	☐	☐

6. PLAYING WITH DOLLS

Put an ordinary doll in front of the child and wait for her reaction.
Put a doll's cup, plate, potty, brush and blanket next to the doll and wait
again for the child's reaction.

1. The child takes the initiative to play with the doll.
   Describe how

   . . . .
   . . . .
   . . . .

	YES	NO
2. The child begins of its own initiative to play with the doll's toys.	☐	☐
3. Other.	☐	☐

Stimulate the child's interest by initiating a short sequence of action (script)
with the doll. (It is morning: first the doll gets up, then it needs to use the potty,
eats breakfast etc.)

	YES	NO
1. The child recognizes the script and initiates further actions.	☐	☐

   Describe how (by function / by pretending)

   . . . .

2. The child imitates the adult's actions without initiating any further actions.	☐	☐

   Describe which of the adult's acts

   . . . .

3. The child shows no interest in the doll at all.	☐	☐

Common features of early development

Here we summarize some of the features of early development which are important to play, communication and social interaction.

0 months

Innate reactions and patterns of attention.
Sensitivity and reflex movements.

2 months

Activity is not only determined by innate patterns of reaction.
Clear distinction between behaviour related to things and people.
Qualified eye contact.
Social smile.

6 months

Attention to other people's reactions.
Reaches out and expects to be picked up.
Repeats actions and imitates other people.
Carries out simple play rituals with one thing at a time.
Looks at own image (in a mirror).

9 months

Joint and shared attention.
Affective attunement in relation to the environment.
Smiles towards or plays with own image (in a mirror).
Object persistence – remembers things not in view.
Combination play rituals with more things at a time.

13 months

Combination play is developed into functional play.

Can play 'pat-a-cake', horse-riding on an adult's knee, etc (script and expectation).

Passes things when encouraged – gives and takes when playing games with turn-taking.

Knows own name.

18 months

Uses pretend play, such as pretending that a doll is alive.

Develops small play themes based on daily routines (scripts).

Plays in a parallel way together with other children.

Shows, offers and takes toys.

24 months

The doll is the passive recipient of the child's care and the actions are familiar to the child from her own daily life (changing nappies, putting to bed, getting fed etc).

36 months

The doll is gradually ascribed with its own needs (ie wants a coke rather than milk).

Understands that different people have different needs.

48 months

Actual role play, where different dolls are given different roles and personalities – play has an inner drama.

Play reflects the child's ability to create mental images ('theory of mind').

The age groups given in the outline refer to normal development, so appropriate allowances should be made for this.

Bibliography

Astington, J.W. and Olson, D.R. (1988) *Developing Theories of Mind.* Cambridge: Cambridge University Press.

Baron-Cohen, S. Leslie, Firth (1985) 'Does the autistic child have a "theory of mind"?' *Cognition 21,* 37–46.

Baron-Cohen, S. (1987) 'Autism and symbolic play.' *British Journal of Developmental Psychology 5,* 139–148.

Baron-Cohen, S. (1988) 'Social and pragmatic deficits in autism: Cognitive or affective.' *Journal of Autism and Developmental Disorders 18,* 3, 379–402.

Baron-Cohen, S. (1989) 'The theory of mind hypothesis of autism: A reply to Boucher.' *British Journal of Disorders of Communication 24,* 199–200.

Baron-Cohen, S. Tager-Flusberg, H. and Cohen, D. (eds) (1993) *Understanding Other Minds.* Oxford: Oxford University Press.

Berckelaer-Onnes, I. 'Play training for autistic children.' In J. Hellendoorn and R. der Kooij (eds) (1997) *Play and Intervention.* SUNY series, Children's Play in Society. Albany, New York: State University of New York Press.

Beyer, J. (1992) *Autisme og Udvikling 3* opgave. Copenhagen: Autism and Development DLH.

Bourcher, J. (1989) 'The theory of mind hypothesis of autism: Explanation, evidence and assessment.' *British Journal of Disorders of Communication 24,* 181–198.

Broström, S. (1997) 'Children's play: Tools and symbols in frame play.' *Early Years 17,* 2, 16-21.

Elkonin, D. (1989) *Legens Psykologi (The Psychology of Play).* Artikel 1997. Elkonin. D. (1989) *Autisme – En Gådes Afklaring.* Copenhagen: Hans Reitzels Forlag.

Emde *et al.* (1978) 'Emotional expression in infancy: II. early deviations in Down's Syndrome.' In Lewis and Rosenblum (eds) *The Development of Affect.* New York and London.

Frith, U. (1989) *Autism - Explaning the Enigma.* Oxford: Basil Blackwell Ltd.

Gillberg, C. (1995) *Clinical Child Neuropsychiatry.* Cambridge: Cambridge University Press.

Gould, J. (1986) 'The Lowe and Costello symbolic play test.' *Journal of Autism and Developmental Disorders 16*, 199–213.

Gray, C.A. (1995) 'Teaching children with autism to "read" social situations.' In K.A. Quill (ed) *Teaching Children with Autism: Strategies to Enhance Communication and Socialization.* Albany, New York: Delmar Publishers Inc.

Happé, F. (1994) *Autism: An Introduction to Psychological Theory.* London: UCL Press Limited

Happé, F. (1995) *Autisme.* Copenhagen: Hans Reitzels Forlag.

Harris, P.L. (1994) *Børn og Følelser.* Copenhagen: Hans Reitzels Forlag.

Harris, P.L. (1989) *Children and Emotion.* Oxford: Basil Blackwell Ltd.

Hobson, R.P. (1989) 'Beyond cognition – a theory of autism.' In G. Dawson (ed) *Autism: Nature, Diagnosis, and Treatment.* New York and London: Guildford Press.

Hobson, R.P. (1990) 'On acquiring knowledge about people and the capacity to pretend: Response to Leslie.' *Psychological Review 97*, 1, 114–121.

Hobson, R.P. (1993) *Autism and the Development of Mind.* Hillsdale, New Jersey: Lawrence Erlbaum Associates.

Hoffman, M. (1981) 'Perspectives on the difference between understanding people and understanding things.' In Flavell and Ross (eds) *Social Cognitive Development.* Cambridge: Cambridge University Press.

Kanner, L. (1943) 'Autistic disturbances of affective contact.' *Nervous Child 2*, 217–50.

Kasari, C., Sigman, M., Mundy, P. and Yirmiya, N. (1990) 'Affective sharing in the context of joint attention interactions of normal, autistic and mentally retarded children.' *Journal of Autism and Developmental Disorders 20*, 1, 87–100.

Leslie, A.M. (1987) 'Pretense and representation: The origins of "theory of mind".' *Psychological Review 94*, 412–26.

Leslie, A.M. and Frith, U. (1990) 'Prospects for a cognitive neuropsychology of autism: Hobson's choice. *Psychological Review 97,* 1, 122-131.

Lord, Catherine; Rutter, Michael; Di Lavore, Pamela (1995) Autism Diagnostic Observation. Schedule - Generic (ADOS)

Mundy, P. and Sigman, M. (1989) 'Specifying the nature of the social impairment in autism.' In G. Dawson (ed) *Autism: Nature, Diagnosis and Treatment.* New York and London: Guildford Press.

Mundy, P., Sigman, M. and Kasari, C. (1990) 'A longitudinal study of joint attention and language development in autistic children.' *Journal of Autism and Developmental Disorders 20,* 1 115–128.

Nelson, K. and Seidman, S. (1984) 'Playing with scripts.' In I. Bretherton (ed) *Symbolic Play.* New York: Academic Press.

Nelson, K. (ed) (1986) *Event Knowledge.* Lawrence Earlbaum Associates.

O'connor (ed) *Language, Cognitive Deficits, and Retardation.* (pp. 75–80), Oxford: Butterworths.

Peeters, Theo (1997) *Autism: From Theoretical Understanding to Educational Intervention.* London: Whurr.

Piaget, J. (1962) *Play, Dreams and Imitation in Childhood.* London: Routledge and Kegan Paul.

Ricks, D.M. (1975) 'Vocal communication in pre-verbal normal and autistic children.' In O'Connor (ed) *Language, Cognitive Deficits and Retardation.* Oxford: Butterworths.

Ricks, D.M. and Wing, L. (1975) 'Language, communication and the use of symbols in normal and autistic children.' *Journal of Autism and Childhood Schizophrenia 5,* 191–221.

Ricks, D.M. (1979) 'Making sense of experience to make sensible sounds.' In B. Margaret (ed) *Before Speech.* Cambridge: Cambridge University Press.

Schopler, E. and Mesibov, G. (ed) (1995) *Learning and Cognition in Autism.* New York: Plenum Press.

Stern, D. (1985) *The Interpersonal World of the Infant.* New York: Basic Books.

Stern, D. (1995) *The Motherhood Constellation.* New York: Basic Books.

Tager-Flusberg, H. (1989) 'A psycholinguistic perspective on language development in the autistic child.' In G. Dawson (ed) *Autism – Nature, Diagnosis and Treatment.*

Trevarthen, C. (1978) 'Secondary intersubjectivity.' L. Andrew (ed) *Action, Gesture and Symbol.* New York: Academic Press.

Trevarthen, C. (1979) 'Communication and cooperation in early infancy.' In G. Margaret (ed) *Before Speech.* Cambridge: Cambridge University Press.

Trevarthen, C., Aitken, K., Papoudi, D. and Robarts, J. (1996) *Children with Autism.* London: Jessica Kingsley Publishers.

Trillingsgaard, A. (1999) 'The script model in relation to autism.' *European Child and Adolescent Psychiatry 8*, 45–49.

Waterhouse and Fein (1989) 'Social or cognitive or both? Crucial dysfunctions in autism.' In C. Gillberg (ed) *Diagnosis and Treatment of Autism.* New York: Plenum Press.

Wing, L., Gould, J., Yeates, S.R. and Brierley, L.M. (1977) 'Symbolic play in severely mentally retarded and in autistic children.' *Journal of Autism and Developmental Disorders 15*, 139–148.

Wing, L. (1997) *The Autistic Spectrum.* Constable and Company Limited.

Wolfberg, P. (1995) 'Enhancing children's play.' In K.A. Quill (ed) *Teaching Children with Autism: Strategies to Enhance Communication and Socialization.* Albany, New York: Delmar Publishers Inc.